Beyond Comfort Zone

- The Path to Personal Growth

Badarinath Devarasetty

DEDICATION

This book is dedicated to Praveena Devarasetty, the girl of my dreams. After our marriage we have been living dream together.

I canot imagine my life without her.

ACKNOWLEDGMENTS

CONTENTS

Introduction

Do you feel like you're stuck in a rut, going through the motions of life without experiencing any real growth or progress? Are you afraid to take risks or step outside of your comfort zone? If so, you're not alone. Many people find themselves in this position, feeling unfulfilled and uncertain about how to move forward.

But what if I told you that the key to personal growth and fulfillment lies in stepping beyond your comfort zone? In this book, we'll explore why it's important to challenge yourself and take risks, even when it's scary. We'll look at the benefits of stepping outside your comfort zone, and we'll provide practical tips and strategies for doing so.

Through inspiring stories and actionable advice, you'll learn how to break free from the limitations that are holding you back, and start living the life you've always dreamed of. It won't be easy, but the journey to personal growth is always worth it.

Stepping out of your comfort zone can be a daunting task, but it's essential for personal growth and development. When we stay within our comfort zone, we limit ourselves and miss out on opportunities for learning, exploring new experiences, and achieving our full potential.

Going beyond our comfort zone means taking risks, trying new things, and facing our fears. It's about pushing ourselves out of our familiar routine and challenging ourselves to do things we might not have thought possible.

One of the most significant benefits of stepping out of our comfort zone is the personal growth and development that comes with it. By facing new challenges and experiences, we learn more about ourselves, our strengths and weaknesses, and what we are capable of achieving.

Stepping out of our comfort zone can also lead to increased confidence and self-esteem. When we achieve something we previously thought was impossible, we feel a sense of accomplishment and pride in ourselves. This, in turn, can motivate us to continue to take risks and pursue our goals..

So, whether it's trying a new hobby, taking a new course, or starting a new job, stepping out of our comfort zone can bring significant benefits to our lives. It may be uncomfortable and challenging at first, but in the end, it's worth it for the personal growth and development it brings. .

Chapter 1: What is a Comfort Zone?

Most of us have heard of the term "comfort zone," but what does it actually mean? Your comfort zone is a psychological state where you feel safe, secure, and in control. It's a place where you're familiar with your surroundings and know what to expect. In this state, you're not likely to experience much anxiety, stress, or fear.

While it might seem like a desirable place to be, staying in your comfort zone for too long can actually hinder your personal growth. When you're not challenged or pushed outside of your limits, you're not growing or developing new skills. You're simply maintaining the status quo.

A comfort zone is a place of familiarity, a space where you feel at ease and in control. It's where you know what to expect, where you feel secure and safe. It's that space where you don't have to challenge yourself, where you don't have to push beyond your limits or face your fears.

It's easy to fall into the comfort zone trap, to stick with what we know and avoid anything that could disrupt our sense of security. However, staying in our comfort zone can also limit our growth and potential. We may miss out on new opportunities, experiences, and relationships that can help us expand and learn.

Comfort zones can manifest in various aspects of our lives, including work, relationships, and hobbies. For example, you may have a job that you're good at, but it doesn't challenge you or offer room for growth. You may stay in a relationship that's comfortable, but doesn't fulfill you emotionally or intellectually. Or, you may stick with familiar hobbies that don't challenge you to learn new skills or step out of your comfort zone.

Stepping out of our comfort zone can be scary and challenging, but it's also where growth and change happen. It's where we can discover new abilities and strengths, face our fears, and develop resilience. By challenging ourselves and pushing beyond our limits, we can expand our comfort zone and discover new possibilities.

A comfort zone is a psychological state in which an individual feels safe, secure, and at ease with their surroundings and the tasks they are performing. It is a familiar and comfortable place where people feel in control and have a sense of predictability. In this zone, individuals are not usually challenged, and they may feel resistant or hesitant to step outside of it.

Comfort zones can be beneficial, as they provide a sense of stability and reduce stress levels. However, they can also be limiting, as individuals may miss out on opportunities for growth and development by staying within their comfort zone. Stepping outside of one's comfort zone can be uncomfortable and may involve risk, but it can also lead to personal and professional growth, new experiences, and greater self-confidence.

Stepping out of one's comfort zone can involve trying new things, taking on new challenges, and facing fears and uncertainties. It requires a willingness to take risks and tolerate the discomfort that comes with the unknown. However, it can also lead to a sense of accomplishment and self-efficacy when individuals succeed in these new experiences.

Many people may feel stuck in their comfort zones, whether it be in their personal or professional lives. They may be hesitant to take on new challenges or try new things, fearing failure or embarrassment. However, it's important to remember that growth and learning often occur outside of our comfort zones. By gradually pushing ourselves outside of our comfort zones, we can expand our capabilities, build resilience, and develop new skills.

It's important to note that stepping out of one's comfort zone doesn't mean constantly living in a state of discomfort or anxiety. Rather, it's about finding a balance between challenging ourselves and taking care of our mental health and wellbeing. It's okay to take small steps outside of our comfort zones and to take breaks when necessary.

Overall, while comfort zones can provide a sense of security and stability, they can also limit our potential for growth and development. By stepping outside of our comfort zones and embracing new experiences, we can expand our horizons, build confidence, and achieve personal and professional success.

There are several benefits to stepping outside of our comfort zones. For example, it can lead to increased creativity and innovation. When we are faced with new challenges or experiences, our brains are forced to think in different ways and come up with creative solutions. This can be especially beneficial in the workplace, where creativity and innovation are highly valued.

Stepping outside of our comfort zones can also lead to personal growth and increased self-awareness. When we push ourselves to try new things or take on new challenges, we often discover new strengths and capabilities that we didn't know we had. This can lead to a greater sense of self-confidence and self-efficacy.

Another benefit of stepping outside of our comfort zones is that it can lead to new opportunities and experiences. When we try new things or take on new challenges, we often meet new people and discover new interests. This can lead to a more fulfilling and enriching life.

Of course, stepping outside of our comfort zones can also be difficult and uncomfortable. It's important to be kind to ourselves and to remember that failure is a natural part of the learning process. By embracing a growth mindset and focusing on progress rather than perfection, we can continue to push ourselves outside of our comfort zones and achieve our goals.

Comfort zones can provide a sense of security and stability, they can also limit our potential for growth and development. By stepping outside of our comfort zones and embracing new experiences, we can expand our horizons, build confidence, and achieve personal and professional success.

One way to step out of our comfort zones is to set goals that challenge us. These goals should be specific, measurable, and achievable, but also push us beyond what we think we are capable of. By setting challenging goals, we can motivate ourselves to take action and work towards personal growth and development.

Another way to step out of our comfort zones is to expose ourselves to new experiences and perspectives. This could involve trying new hobbies, traveling to new places, or engaging in activities outside of our usual routines. By exposing ourselves to new experiences and perspectives, we can broaden our horizons and expand our knowledge and understanding of the world around us.

It's also important to remember that stepping outside of our comfort zones is a process that takes time and effort. It's not always easy, and setbacks and failures are inevitable. However, by persevering through these challenges and continuing to push ourselves, we can achieve our goals and become the best version of ourselves.

It's also important to seek support and encouragement from

those around us when we're stepping outside of our comfort zones. This could include friends, family, colleagues, or a mentor. Having a support system can provide us with the motivation and encouragement we need to keep pushing ourselves towards our goals.

We can develop a growth mindset to help us embrace the challenges that come with stepping outside of our comfort zones. A growth mindset involves believing that our abilities and talents can be developed through hard work and dedication. It's about seeing failures and setbacks as opportunities for growth and learning, rather than as indications of our limitations.

It's important to take care of ourselves as we step outside of our comfort zones. This means practicing self-care and self-compassion, and recognizing when we need to take a break or seek support. By prioritizing our mental and physical wellbeing, we can continue to push ourselves towards our goals while maintaining a healthy balance in our lives.

Another important aspect of stepping outside of our comfort zones is being open to feedback and learning from our experiences. Feedback can help us identify areas for improvement and make adjustments to our approach. It's important to be open to feedback, even if it's difficult to hear, and to use it as an opportunity to grow and improve.

Additionally, stepping outside of our comfort zones can involve taking on leadership roles or challenging ourselves in our careers. This may involve taking on new responsibilities or pursuing a new career path. By stepping outside of our comfort zones in our professional lives, we can expand our skill sets, take on new challenges, and grow as professionals.

It's also important to remember that stepping outside of our comfort zones is not a one-time event, but an ongoing process. As we achieve our goals and gain new experiences, we may need to continue pushing ourselves to grow and develop. It's important to maintain a growth mindset and remain open to new opportunities and challenges.

Overall, stepping outside of our comfort zones can be challenging, but it's an essential part of personal and professional growth and development. By being open to feedback, taking on new challenges, pursuing leadership roles, and maintaining a growth mindset, we can continue to push ourselves towards our full potential and achieve success in all areas of our lives.

In conclusion, stepping outside of our comfort zones can be challenging, but it's essential for personal and professional growth and development. While it can be uncomfortable and challenging, it can also lead to increased creativity, self-awareness, and new opportunities. By setting challenging goals, exposing ourselves to new experiences, seeking support and encouragement, developing a growth mindset, and taking care of ourselves, we can continue to push ourselves towards our full potential. A comfort zone is a familiar and safe space where we feel secure, but it can also limit our growth and potential. Stepping out of our comfort zone can be challenging but can lead to growth and new opportunities.

Chapter 2: Why Stepping Outside Your Comfort Zone is Important

Stepping outside your comfort zone is essential if you want to experience personal growth and develop new skills. When you take on new challenges and push yourself to try new things, you're building resilience, confidence, and self-esteem. You're also learning from your mistakes and developing problem-solving skills that will serve you well in all areas of your life.

Stepping outside of your comfort zone can be a daunting task. It requires taking risks and facing fears that may have been holding you back. However, the benefits of doing so are immense and can lead to personal growth and new opportunities that may not have been possible within the confines of your comfort zone.

When you stay within your comfort zone, you limit yourself to what you already know and what feels safe. This can result in missed opportunities for growth and success, both personally and professionally. By stepping outside of your comfort zone, you are opening yourself up to new experiences and challenges that can help you learn and develop new skills.

Additionally, stepping outside of your comfort zone can help you build resilience and confidence. When you face your fears and overcome challenges, you prove to yourself that you are capable of achieving more than you thought possible. This, in turn, can help you feel more confident in yourself and your abilities.

It's important to note that stepping outside of your comfort zone doesn't mean taking reckless risks or putting yourself in dangerous situations. It means taking calculated risks that challenge you and push you to grow. This may involve trying new things, taking on new responsibilities, or putting yourself in social situations that make you uncomfortable.

In relationships, stepping outside of your comfort zone can also be beneficial. It can help you to communicate more effectively, resolve conflicts, and deepen connections with others. By being open to new experiences and perspectives, you can also gain a better understanding of others and their needs, which can help to strengthen your relationships.

Stepping outside your comfort zone is important for several reasons. First, it allows you to challenge yourself and push your limits, which can help you grow and develop as a person. When you step outside your comfort zone, you are forced to confront new situations and experiences, which can help you build resilience and develop new skills.

Second, stepping outside your comfort zone can lead to new opportunities and experiences that you might not have otherwise had. When you try new things and take risks, you open yourself up to a world of possibilities that you might not have known existed. This can lead to personal and professional growth, as well as increased confidence and self-esteem.

Third, stepping outside your comfort zone can help you overcome fear and anxiety. When we stay within our comfort zones, we tend to avoid situations that make us feel uncomfortable or anxious. However, when we face these situations head-on, we can learn to manage our fear and anxiety, which can lead to increased confidence and resilience.

Finally, stepping outside your comfort zone can help you break out of old habits and patterns of behavior. When we stay within our comfort zones, we tend to stick to familiar routines and habits. However, when we challenge ourselves and try new things, we can break out of these old patterns and develop new and healthier habits.

In addition to the benefits mentioned above, stepping outside your comfort zone can also lead to increased creativity and innovation. When you challenge yourself to think differently and approach problems from new angles, you can unlock new insights and ideas that you might not have otherwise considered. This can be particularly valuable in professional settings, where innovative thinking and problem-solving skills are highly valued.

Furthermore, stepping outside your comfort zone can help you build stronger relationships with others. When you try new things and take risks, you demonstrate a willingness to be vulnerable and open to new experiences. This can help you connect with others on a deeper level and build trust and rapport.

It's important to note that stepping outside your comfort zone doesn't necessarily mean taking huge risks or making drastic changes in your life. It can be as simple as trying a new hobby, taking on a new project at work, or striking up a conversation with someone you don't know. The key is to challenge yourself to do something that feels uncomfortable or unfamiliar.

It's worth noting that stepping outside your comfort zone can be scary and uncomfortable. It's natural to feel anxious or uncertain when facing new challenges or situations. However, it's important to remember that discomfort and fear are often signs that you're growing and pushing yourself in new directions. With time and practice, you can learn to manage these feelings and continue to push yourself towards your goals.

Overall, stepping outside your comfort zone is important for personal and professional growth, innovation, and building stronger relationships with others. By challenging yourself to try new things and take risks, you can unlock new opportunities and experiences and reach your full potential.

It's important to note that stepping outside your comfort zone should be a gradual process, and not something that you force yourself to do all at once. It's okay to start small and gradually build up to bigger challenges as you become more comfortable with stepping outside your comfort zone.

It's also important to be kind and patient with yourself as you navigate this process. Stepping outside your comfort zone can be difficult, and it's natural to experience setbacks or challenges along the way. However, it's important to remember that growth and progress are not always linear, and that every step you take towards your goals is an important one.

Finally, it's important to surround yourself with supportive people who encourage and inspire you to step outside your comfort zone. Whether it's friends, family members, or colleagues, having a support system can make all the difference in your journey towards personal and professional growth.

Stepping outside your comfort zone is important for personal and professional growth, innovation, and building stronger relationships with others. It allows you to challenge yourself, push your limits, and develop new skills and habits. It can also lead to new opportunities and experiences, increased confidence and self-esteem, and the ability to manage fear and anxiety.

While stepping outside your comfort zone can be scary and uncomfortable, it's important to remember that growth and progress often come from discomfort and facing new challenges. Starting small and gradually building up to bigger challenges can help you navigate this process, as can surrounding yourself with supportive people who encourage and inspire you.

By embracing new experiences, taking risks, and challenging yourself, you can unlock your full potential and achieve success in all areas of your life. So don't be afraid to step outside your comfort zone and try something new - you never know what opportunities and experiences might be waiting for you.

Whether in your personal or professional life, challenging yourself to take calculated risks can be a powerful tool for achieving your goals and living a more fulfilling life. You can build resilience, develop new skills, and open yourself up to a world of possibilities.

In conclusion, while it can be scary to step outside of your comfort zone, doing so can lead to personal growth, increased confidence, and new opportunities. Stepping outside your comfort zone is an important part of personal and professional growth and development. By challenging yourself to try new things, take risks, and confront new situations and experiences, you can unlock new opportunities, build resilience, and reach your full potential. While stepping outside your comfort zone can be difficult and uncomfortable, it's important to remember that every step you take towards your goals is an important one. With patience, perseverance, and support, you can continue to push yourself towards your goals and achieve success in all areas of your life.

Chapter 3: The Benefits of Stepping Outside Your Comfort Zone

There are many benefits to stepping outside your comfort zone. You'll experience personal growth, develop new skills, and build resilience and confidence. You'll also become more adaptable and flexible, which will help you to deal with unexpected challenges and changes in your life.

Stepping outside your comfort zone can bring numerous benefits to your life. Here are some of them:

1. Personal growth: When you step outside your comfort zone, you challenge yourself to try new things and take risks. This can lead to personal growth and a greater sense of self-confidence.

2. Expanded horizons: By trying new things, you expose yourself to different experiences and perspectives. This can broaden your horizons and help you see the world in a new way.

3. Increased creativity: When you step outside your

comfort zone, you are forced to think creatively and come up with new solutions to problems. This can lead to increased creativity in other areas of your life.

4. Enhanced learning: Trying new things and taking on new challenges can help you learn and develop new skills. This can lead to personal and professional growth.

5. Overcoming fear: Often, our comfort zone is limited by our fears. Stepping outside of it can help us overcome those fears and develop greater courage and resilience.

6. Improved mental health: Trying new things and challenging yourself can lead to a sense of accomplishment and greater self-esteem, which can improve your overall mental health.

7. New opportunities: Stepping outside of your comfort zone can also open up new opportunities for you. By trying new things and expanding your horizons, you may meet new people, discover new passions, and find new career paths that you never would have considered before.

8. Resilience: When you step outside of your comfort zone, you may encounter setbacks and failures. However, these experiences can help you develop

resilience and the ability to bounce back from challenges.

9. Increased adaptability: When you challenge yourself to try new things and take on new challenges, you become more adaptable and flexible. This can be a valuable skill in both your personal and professional life.

10. Breaking out of routine: Stepping outside of your comfort zone can help you break out of your routine and experience new things. This can help you avoid getting stuck in a rut and feeling stagnant in your life.

11. Greater self-awareness: When you step outside of your comfort zone, you may discover new things about yourself. You may learn that you have strengths you never knew existed or uncover areas where you need to improve. This increased self-awareness can help you make better decisions and live a more fulfilling life.

12. Building relationships: Trying new things and taking on new challenges can also help you build stronger relationships with others. By sharing experiences and facing challenges together, you can develop deeper connections with those around you.

13. Sense of accomplishment: Stepping outside of your

comfort zone can give you a sense of accomplishment and pride in yourself. When you overcome a fear or achieve a goal that once seemed impossible, you can feel a sense of satisfaction and confidence that can carry over into other areas of your life.

14. Setting an example: When you step outside of your comfort zone, you can inspire others to do the same. By demonstrating that it's possible to try new things and take risks, you can encourage others to do the same and live a more fulfilling life.

15. Overcoming self-limiting beliefs: Stepping outside of your comfort zone can help you overcome self-limiting beliefs that may be holding you back. By challenging yourself to try new things and take on new challenges, you can prove to yourself that you are capable of more than you thought.

16. Increased motivation: When you step outside of your comfort zone and achieve something new, it can increase your motivation to keep pushing yourself further. This can help you set new goals and work towards them with renewed energy and enthusiasm.

17. Developing a growth mindset: Stepping outside of your comfort zone can help you develop a growth mindset, where you believe that your abilities and

skills can be developed through hard work and dedication. This can lead to a more positive outlook on life and a greater willingness to take on new challenges.

18. Greater sense of purpose: When you challenge yourself to try new things and take on new challenges, it can give you a greater sense of purpose and direction in life. By pursuing new experiences and goals, you can find a deeper meaning and fulfillment in your life.

19. Developing resilience: Stepping outside of your comfort zone can help you develop resilience, which is the ability to bounce back from setbacks and challenges. This can be a valuable skill in both your personal and professional life, helping you to overcome obstacles and achieve your goals.

20. Living life to the fullest: Ultimately, stepping outside of your comfort zone can help you live life to the fullest. By embracing new experiences and taking on new challenges, you can create a life that is rich, fulfilling, and full of meaning.

Stepping outside your comfort zone can be a daunting task, but it can also bring about a plethora of benefits. It allows you to push yourself to grow and develop as an individual. When you take risks and try new things, you open yourself up to new experiences and opportunities.

One of the most significant benefits of stepping outside your comfort zone is personal growth. When you challenge yourself and try new things, you learn more about yourself and your capabilities. You may discover hidden talents or interests you never knew you had. By pushing yourself out of your comfort zone, you can improve your confidence and self-esteem, as you prove to yourself that you are capable of achieving more than you thought possible.

Another benefit of stepping outside your comfort zone is the opportunity to expand your knowledge and skills. When you try new things, you expose yourself to new information and experiences that can broaden your horizons. This can lead to increased creativity and innovation, as well as improved problem-solving abilities.

Stepping outside your comfort zone can also help you to break free from limiting beliefs and thought patterns. Often, our comfort zones are defined by our fears and anxieties. By facing and overcoming these fears, you can expand your comfort zone and break free from the limiting beliefs that hold you back. This can lead to increased resilience and adaptability, which can serve you well in both personal and professional situations.

In summary, there are many benefits to stepping outside of your comfort zone. From personal growth and expanded horizons to improved mental health and greater resilience, challenging yourself to try new things can lead to a more fulfilling and rewarding life. So, don't be afraid to take a chance and try something new today! While it can be scary to step outside of your comfort zone, doing so can bring many benefits to your life. Whether it's trying a new hobby, taking on a new job, or traveling to a new place, pushing yourself to try new things can lead to personal growth, expanded horizons, increased creativity, enhanced learning, overcoming fear, and improved mental health.

You never know where it might lead you! Stepping outside your comfort zone can lead to a sense of fulfillment and see how far it can take you on your personal and professional journey.

Chapter 4: Overcoming Fear and Resistance

One of the biggest barriers to stepping outside your comfort zone is fear. Fear can be a powerful motivator, but it can also hold you back from achieving your goals. In this chapter, we'll look at how to overcome fear and resistance, and how to develop the courage and confidence to take on new challenges.

Fear and resistance are two major obstacles that can prevent us from stepping outside our comfort zone. They can hold us back from taking risks, trying new things, and pursuing our dreams. However, if we learn to overcome them, we can unlock our full potential and achieve greater success in all areas of our lives.

One effective way to overcome fear and resistance is to face them head-on. This means acknowledging your fears and resistance, understanding where they come from, and then taking action to overcome them. It may not be easy, but it is necessary if you want to grow and achieve your goals.

Overcoming fear and resistance is an essential part of stepping outside your comfort zone. Fear and resistance can hold you back from trying new things, taking risks, and pursuing your goals. Here are some tips to help you overcome fear and resistance:

1. Recognize your fears: The first step in overcoming fear and resistance is to recognize them. Take some time to identify the things that scare you or make you feel uncomfortable. By understanding your fears, you can begin to address them.

2. Challenge your fears: Once you've identified your fears, challenge them. Ask yourself whether your fears are realistic and whether they are based on facts or assumptions. Try to see things from a different perspective and consider the potential benefits of taking a risk.

3. Start small: If you're feeling overwhelmed by the idea of stepping outside your comfort zone, start small. Take on small challenges that push you out of your comfort zone but don't feel too daunting. As you build your confidence, you can tackle bigger challenges.

4. Take action: The best way to overcome fear and resistance is to take action. Don't wait for the perfect moment or until you feel completely ready. Start

taking small steps towards your goal, even if they feel scary or uncomfortable.

5. Celebrate your progress: Celebrate your progress, no matter how small it may seem. Acknowledge your efforts and the progress you've made, and use that as motivation to keep pushing yourself further.

6. Practice self-care: It's important to take care of yourself as you step outside your comfort zone. Practice self-care by getting enough sleep, eating well, exercising, and taking time to relax and recharge.

7. Seek support: Finally, don't be afraid to seek support from others. Surround yourself with people who encourage and support you, and who believe in your ability to succeed. You may also consider working with a therapist or coach who can help you work through your fears and develop strategies for overcoming them.

8. Learn from failures: It's important to remember that failure is a natural part of taking risks and stepping outside your comfort zone. Instead of letting failures discourage you, use them as an opportunity to learn

and grow. Take the lessons you've learned from your failures and use them to make better decisions in the future.

9. Embrace uncertainty: When you step outside your comfort zone, there is often a sense of uncertainty and unpredictability. Instead of letting this uncertainty hold you back, embrace it. Remember that uncertainty is a natural part of growth and change, and that it can lead to exciting new opportunities.

10. Stay focused on your goals: When faced with fear and resistance, it can be easy to lose sight of your goals. Stay focused on what you want to achieve and use that as motivation to push through your fears and take action.

11. Reframe your mindset: Reframe your mindset to focus on the positive aspects of stepping outside your comfort zone. Instead of focusing on the potential risks and negative outcomes, focus on the potential rewards and positive outcomes that can come from taking a risk.

12. Take calculated risks: While it's important to take risks in order to step outside your comfort zone, it's

also important to take calculated risks. This means weighing the potential risks and benefits of a decision and making an informed choice.

13. Be patient with yourself: Stepping outside your comfort zone can be a challenging and sometimes slow process. Be patient with yourself and celebrate small successes along the way.

14. Practice gratitude: Practicing gratitude can help shift your focus from fear and resistance to a more positive mindset. Take time each day to reflect on the things you're grateful for, and use that as motivation to keep pushing yourself outside your comfort zone.

15. Visualize success: Visualization is a powerful tool for overcoming fear and resistance. Take some time to visualize yourself successfully stepping outside your comfort zone and achieving your goals. This can help you build confidence and stay motivated.

16. Set realistic expectations: It's important to set realistic expectations for yourself when stepping outside your comfort zone. Don't expect perfection or overnight success. Instead, focus on making progress and celebrating small wins along the way.

17. Stay open-minded: Stepping outside your comfort zone often involves encountering new and unfamiliar experiences. Stay open-minded and embrace new ideas and perspectives. This can help you grow and learn in ways you never imagined.

18. Practice mindfulness: Mindfulness can help you stay present and focused as you step outside your comfort zone. Take some time each day to practice mindfulness, whether it's through meditation, deep breathing, or simply being present in the moment.

19. Believe in yourself: Finally, the most important factor in overcoming fear and resistance is believing in yourself. Trust in your abilities and your capacity to handle challenges and uncertainty. With self-belief, anything is possible.

20. Surround yourself with support: Having a support system can make all the difference when stepping outside your comfort zone. Surround yourself with people who believe in you and support your goals. They can provide encouragement and help you stay accountable as you face your fears.

21. Celebrate your achievements: Celebrating your achievements, no matter how small, can help you stay motivated and build confidence. Take the time to acknowledge your progress and celebrate your successes along the way.

22. Reflect on your experiences: After taking a risk and stepping outside your comfort zone, take some time to reflect on your experiences. What did you learn? What challenges did you face? How did you grow as a result? Reflection can help you gain insight and perspective on your journey.

23. Keep pushing yourself: Stepping outside your comfort zone is not a one-time event, but an ongoing process. Keep pushing yourself to take new risks and try new things. This can help you continue to grow and develop in all areas of your life.

24. Celebrate the process: Finally, remember that stepping outside your comfort zone is not just about achieving a goal, but also about the journey itself. Celebrate the process of growth and self-discovery, and enjoy the excitement and challenge of stepping into the unknown.

By incorporating these tips into your life, you can overcome fear and resistance, and discover the incredible rewards of stepping outside your comfort zone. So take a deep breath, take that first step, and start your journey towards personal growth and success.

By facing your fears and resistance, you can learn to overcome them and achieve greater success in all areas of your life. Remember, it's not about being fearless, it's about having the courage to face your fears and take action anyway.

In conclusion, overcoming fear and resistance is essential for stepping outside your comfort zone and achieving your goals. By recognizing your fears, challenging them, starting small, taking action, celebrating your progress, practicing self-care, and seeking support, you can overcome your fears and achieve success.

The rewards of stepping outside your comfort zone are truly worth the effort.

Chapter 5: Setting Realistic Goals

Setting realistic goals is an essential part of stepping outside your comfort zone. In this chapter, we'll look at how to set goals that are challenging but achievable, and how to break them down into smaller, manageable steps.

Setting goals is an essential step towards achieving success in any aspect of life. However, it is important to set realistic goals that are achievable and within your reach. Setting unrealistic goals can lead to disappointment, frustration, and even failure.

When setting goals, it is important to assess your abilities and resources realistically. This means taking into consideration your strengths, weaknesses, opportunities, and limitations. You should also consider the external factors that may affect your ability to achieve your goals. These may include economic conditions, social factors, and other circumstances that may be beyond your control.

To set realistic goals, it is important to define them clearly and specifically. This means identifying what you want to achieve, when you want to achieve it, and what steps you need to take to get there. You should also break down your goals into smaller, achievable tasks that you can work on daily or weekly. This will help you stay focused and motivated as you work towards your larger goals.

It is also important to stay flexible and adaptable when setting goals. As you work towards achieving your goals, you may encounter unexpected challenges or setbacks that require you to adjust your plan. In such situations, it is important to remain open to new ideas and approaches that can help you overcome these obstacles and stay on track towards achieving your goals.

Setting realistic goals is important to help you come out of your comfort zone because it allows you to take steps towards achieving something that is attainable yet challenging. When you set goals that are too lofty or unrealistic, you may become overwhelmed or discouraged, which can cause you to revert back to your comfort zone.

On the other hand, setting realistic goals can help you gradually expand your comfort zone and push yourself to grow and improve. These goals can help you identify areas where you need to work on and develop the skills necessary to achieve them. As you accomplish these goals, you gain confidence and a sense of accomplishment, which motivates you to continue setting and achieving more challenging goals.

Furthermore, setting realistic goals can also help you develop a growth mindset, where you view challenges as opportunities for learning and growth rather than as obstacles to avoid. This mindset can help you approach new situations with a positive attitude and a willingness to take risks, which is essential for personal and professional growth.

Moreover, when you set realistic goals, you are also more likely to create an actionable plan to achieve them. This plan will include specific steps that you need to take to reach your goal, as well as deadlines to keep you accountable. By breaking down your goal into smaller, achievable steps, you can avoid feeling overwhelmed or stuck in the process.

Setting realistic goals also helps you to measure your progress more effectively. By tracking your progress towards your goal, you can identify areas where you need to improve, and adjust your plan accordingly. This feedback loop can help you stay on track and make progress towards your goal, even if you experience setbacks along the way.

Finally, setting realistic goals allows you to celebrate your achievements along the way. When you reach a milestone or accomplish a smaller goal, you can celebrate your progress and feel motivated to continue working towards your larger goal. This positive reinforcement can help you stay committed to your goal and continue to push yourself outside of your comfort zone.

Furthermore, setting realistic goals can also help you develop a sense of purpose and direction in life. It gives you something to strive for and helps you focus your energy and efforts on achieving something meaningful. This sense of purpose can be incredibly motivating and can help you maintain your motivation and commitment even when faced with challenges and setbacks.

Moreover, setting realistic goals can also help you improve your self-esteem and confidence. As you achieve your goals, you prove to yourself that you are capable of accomplishing difficult tasks and taking on new challenges. This sense of accomplishment can help you build your confidence and belief in yourself, which can have a positive impact on all areas of your life.

Finally, setting realistic goals can help you create a growth-oriented mindset, which is essential for personal and professional success. When you embrace a growth mindset, you view challenges as opportunities to learn and grow, rather than as threats to your abilities or self-worth. This mindset can help you develop resilience, perseverance, and adaptability, which are all key traits for success in today's rapidly changing world.

To set realistic goals, it's important to start by identifying what you want to achieve and why it's important to you. Then, break down your goal into smaller, manageable steps, and create a plan that outlines what you need to do to achieve each step. It's also important to set specific, measurable, and time-bound targets for each step, so you can track your progress and stay motivated.

Additionally, it can be helpful to seek support from others as you work towards your goals. This can include friends, family, colleagues, or even a professional coach or mentor. Having a support system can provide you with encouragement, accountability, and guidance, which can be invaluable as you navigate challenges and setbacks.

It's also important to be flexible and adaptable as you work towards your goals. Sometimes, unexpected obstacles or opportunities may arise, and you may need to adjust your plan accordingly. By remaining open-minded and willing to adapt, you can stay focused on your ultimate goal while also being responsive to changing circumstances.

In conclusion, setting realistic goals is an essential component of personal and professional growth. By setting attainable yet challenging goals, creating a plan, seeking support, and remaining flexible, you can come out of your comfort zone and achieve your full potential. So, start by identifying your goals and taking action towards achieving them, and watch as you transform into the best version of yourself.

By assessing your abilities and resources realistically, defining your goals clearly and specifically, breaking them down into achievable tasks, staying flexible and adaptable, and staying focused and motivated, you can overcome any challenges that may arise and achieve your desired outcomes.

Chapter 6: Pushing Your Limits

Pushing your limits is an important part of stepping outside your comfort zone. In this chapter, we'll look at how to identify your limits, and how to gradually push past them in a safe and controlled way.

When was the last time you really pushed yourself to your limits? When was the last time you stepped out of your comfort zone and did something that scared you? Something that made you feel alive and invigorated?

Pushing your limits is one of the most exhilarating experiences you can have. It's a rush of adrenaline and a burst of energy that can leave you feeling alive and unstoppable. It's also an essential part of personal growth and development. If you want to achieve greatness and reach your full potential, you need to be willing to push yourself to your limits.

But why is pushing your limits so important? For one, it helps you develop a sense of resilience and mental toughness. When you push yourself to do something difficult, you build confidence and inner strength. You also learn to overcome obstacles and challenges, which is an essential skill in life.

Pushing your limits also helps you break free from limiting beliefs and self-imposed barriers. We often set limits on ourselves based on our past experiences, fears, and doubts.

But when you push yourself to do something that challenges those limits, you prove to yourself that you are capable of more than you thought possible.

Of course, pushing your limits isn't always easy. It can be scary and uncomfortable, and it requires a lot of hard work and dedication. But the rewards are worth it. When you push yourself to your limits, you unlock a whole new level of potential and possibility.

So how do you push yourself to your limits? Start by setting ambitious goals for yourself. Choose something that scares you and that you're not sure you can achieve. Then, break that goal down into smaller, more manageable steps. Focus on each step one at a time, and celebrate your progress along the way.

It's also important to surround yourself with supportive people who believe in you and your ability to push your limits. Seek out mentors and role models who have achieved what you aspire to achieve. Learn from their experiences and let them inspire and motivate you.

Finally, remember that pushing your limits is a journey, not a destination. It's a process of growth and self-discovery that takes time and effort. Embrace the challenges and setbacks along the way, and keep pushing forward.

In the end, pushing your limits is about reaching your full potential and living the life you were meant to live. Don't let fear or self-doubt hold you back. Take a leap of faith and start pushing your limits today.

Pushing your limits refers to challenging yourself to go beyond your comfort zone, to explore your capabilities, and to achieve goals that may seem difficult or impossible at first glance. It involves stepping outside of your comfort zone and taking risks, which can be scary but also incredibly rewarding.

Pushing your limits can come in many forms, such as trying a new activity, taking on a new challenge at work, or setting a personal goal that you've never attempted before. It requires perseverance, determination, and a willingness to embrace failure as a learning opportunity.

By pushing your limits, you can gain confidence in your abilities, discover hidden strengths, and achieve things you never thought possible. It can also help you develop resilience and adaptability, which are essential qualities for personal growth and success.

However, it's important to remember that pushing your limits doesn't mean pushing yourself to the point of exhaustion or burnout. It's essential to listen to your body and mind and take breaks when needed to avoid injury or mental health issues.

Overall, pushing your limits can be a transformative experience that can lead to personal growth, improved self-esteem, and a sense of accomplishment.

When you push your limits, it's important to have a clear goal in mind and to break down the steps needed to achieve that goal. This can help you stay focused and motivated, even when facing obstacles or setbacks along the way.

One effective way to push your limits is to set incremental goals that gradually increase in difficulty. For example, if your goal is to run a marathon, you could start by running a 5K race, then a 10K race, and gradually work your way up to longer distances. This allows you to build confidence and stamina over time, without overwhelming yourself with a challenge that may be too daunting at first.

Another key aspect of pushing your limits is embracing the discomfort and uncertainty that come with taking risks. It's natural to feel fear or anxiety when faced with a new challenge, but these emotions can also be a sign that you're on the right track. By learning to push through these feelings and stay focused on your goal, you can develop a greater sense of resilience and mental toughness.

Of course, it's also important to take care of yourself and avoid pushing your limits to the point of burnout or injury. This means listening to your body, getting enough rest and recovery time, and seeking support from friends, family, or professionals if needed.

Ultimately, pushing your limits can be a powerful way to challenge yourself, grow as a person, and achieve new heights of success and fulfillment. Whether you're pursuing a personal passion, a professional goal, or simply striving to be your best self, the key is to stay focused, stay motivated, and keep pushing forward.

In addition to setting incremental goals and embracing discomfort, another way to push your limits is to seek out feedback and constructive criticism from others. This can help you identify areas for improvement and refine your approach to achieve better results.

It's also important to remember that pushing your limits doesn't always mean going it alone. Building a supportive network of friends, family, or colleagues who share your goals and values can provide valuable encouragement, guidance, and accountability. By working together, you can achieve more than you could on your own and overcome challenges that may have seemed insurmountable.

Finally, pushing your limits is not just about achieving specific goals or milestones. It's also about cultivating a mindset of growth and continuous improvement, even in the face of setbacks or failures. By viewing challenges as opportunities for learning and growth, you can build resilience, adaptability, and a deeper sense of purpose and meaning in your life.

In conclusion, pushing your limits is a powerful way to challenge yourself, grow as a person, and achieve your full potential. By setting clear goals, embracing discomfort, seeking feedback, building a supportive network, and maintaining a growth mindset, you can push past your limits and achieve new levels of success and fulfillment in all areas of your life.

Chapter 7: Embracing Failure

Failure is a natural part of the learning process, but many of us are afraid of it. In this chapter, we'll explore why failure is important, and how to embrace it as a learning opportunity rather than a setback.

Failure is often seen as a negative and painful experience, but it can also be a valuable teacher. Embracing failure means accepting that not every attempt will lead to success, but that each attempt can provide valuable feedback and lessons for future endeavors.

When you step outside your comfort zone and push your limits, failure becomes a more common occurrence. But instead of allowing it to defeat you, you can use it as a tool for growth and improvement. By analyzing the reasons for failure, you can identify areas that need improvement and make necessary changes.

Embracing failure also means letting go of perfectionism and unrealistic expectations. No one is perfect, and expecting yourself to be can lead to unnecessary stress and anxiety. It's important to recognize that failure is a natural part of the learning process and to view it as an opportunity to improve and grow.

In order to embrace failure, it's important to reframe your mindset. Instead of seeing failure as a personal flaw or weakness, view it as an opportunity for growth and development. Recognize that every failure is a step towards success, and that the journey towards achieving your goals may involve setbacks and challenges.

When you embrace failure, you also become more resilient. You develop the ability to bounce back from setbacks and to persevere through difficult times. This resilience can help you to stay focused on your goals, even when faced with obstacles.

Ultimately, embracing failure is about cultivating a growth mindset. By viewing failure as an opportunity to learn and improve, you can approach challenges with confidence and resilience, knowing that every attempt brings you closer to success.

Failure is not the opposite of success, but rather a necessary part of the journey towards achieving it. It is through failure that we learn, grow, and become better equipped to handle the challenges that lie ahead. Embracing failure means acknowledging that it is a natural part of the process, and choosing to learn from it rather than allowing it to defeat us.

One of the biggest obstacles to embracing failure is the fear of what others may think or say. We may worry about being judged, ridiculed, or seen as a failure in the eyes of others. However, it is important to remember that everyone experiences failure at some point in their lives, and that it is through our failures that we often gain the most wisdom and insight.

Another key component of embracing failure is reframing our perspective on what failure actually means. Instead of seeing failure as an endpoint or a reflection of our worth, we can view it as a stepping stone towards success. When we fail, we have the opportunity to reassess our approach, learn from our mistakes, and try again with a newfound understanding of what works and what doesn't.

In order to truly embrace failure, we must also learn to let go of our attachment to perfection. Perfectionism can lead us to become overly self-critical and to place unrealistic expectations on ourselves. By acknowledging that we are all human and that mistakes are inevitable, we can free ourselves from the constraints of perfectionism and allow ourselves to take risks and make mistakes.

Ultimately, embracing failure means adopting a growth mindset, in which we see challenges and setbacks as opportunities for growth and learning. It means being open to feedback, seeking out new experiences, and pushing ourselves to be the best versions of ourselves that we can be. By embracing failure and all that comes with it, we can move closer towards our goals and live a more fulfilling and rewarding life.

Embracing failure means accepting the possibility of not achieving the desired outcome and being willing to learn from mistakes. It is a mindset that encourages experimentation and taking risks, without the fear of making mistakes. By embracing failure, one can develop resilience, perseverance, and a growth mindset, all of which are essential qualities for success in any field.

Rather than viewing failure as a negative outcome, those who embrace it see it as an opportunity to learn and grow. They understand that failure is a natural part of the learning process and that it can provide valuable feedback for improvement. Instead of dwelling on mistakes, they analyze them, identify the causes, and use that information to make adjustments and try again.

Embracing failure can be challenging, especially in a culture that places a high value on success and often stigmatizes failure. However, it is important to recognize that many successful people have experienced failure at some point in their lives. The difference is that they did not let failure define them or stop them from pursuing their goals.

In conclusion, embracing failure requires a shift in mindset, from seeing failure as a negative outcome to viewing it as an opportunity for growth and learning. It is a skill that can be developed through practice and perseverance, and it is essential for achieving success in any area of life.

When one embraces failure, they also become more willing to take risks and try new things. They understand that failure is not the end, but rather a stepping stone on the path to success. This mindset can lead to greater creativity and innovation, as individuals are more willing to think outside the box and try unconventional approaches.

In addition to personal growth, embracing failure can also have positive effects on those around us. When we model a growth mindset and show resilience in the face of failure, we inspire others to do the same. This can create a culture of learning and experimentation, where individuals are encouraged to take risks and learn from their mistakes.

Of course, it's important to note that not all failures are created equal. There are certain failures that can have more severe consequences, and it's important to take responsibility for those failures and learn from them. Embracing failure doesn't mean shirking accountability or failing to learn from our mistakes. Rather, it means acknowledging our mistakes and using them as an opportunity to grow and improve.

In summary, embracing failure is a powerful mindset that can lead to personal and professional growth, as well as greater innovation and creativity. By seeing failure as a natural part of the learning process, we can become more resilient, adaptable, and successful in all areas of our lives.

To truly embrace failure, it's important to let go of the fear of judgment or criticism from others. Often, people are afraid of failure because they worry about what others will think of them if they don't succeed. However, it's important to remember that everyone experiences failure at some point in their lives, and that it's not a reflection of our worth or abilities.

Instead, we should focus on the process of learning and growing, and use failure as an opportunity to improve ourselves. This can involve seeking feedback from others, analyzing our mistakes, and making a plan for how to move forward. It's also important to recognize that failure can sometimes be a necessary step on the path to success. Many successful individuals have experienced failure before achieving their goals, and it's often those failures that teach them the most valuable lessons.

Ultimately, embracing failure requires a mindset shift towards growth and learning. It involves letting go of the fear of failure, taking risks, and being willing to learn from our mistakes. By adopting this mindset, we can become more resilient, creative, and successful in all areas of our lives.

Chapter 8: Developing Resilience

In the face of adversity, resilience is the key to moving forward. It is the ability to bounce back from setbacks, to persevere through difficult times, and to come out stronger on the other side.

Resilience is not something we are born with, but rather it is a skill that can be developed through practice and experience. It involves cultivating a positive mindset, learning to adapt to change, and developing the ability to manage stress and anxiety.

One way to develop resilience is to focus on self-care. This includes taking care of your physical health by eating well, exercising regularly, and getting enough sleep. It also means taking care of your emotional and mental health by practicing mindfulness, meditation, and other relaxation techniques.

Another way to develop resilience is to seek out support from others. This can include talking to a trusted friend or family member, joining a support group, or seeking the help of a mental health professional.

It is important to remember that resilience is not about being invincible or never experiencing hardship. It is about learning to adapt and grow through challenges and setbacks, and coming out stronger and more resilient on the other side. With practice and perseverance, anyone can develop the resilience they need to thrive in the face of adversity.

Resilience is the ability to bounce back from adversity and overcome challenges. It's a crucial trait to have in life, as setbacks and difficulties are inevitable. Developing resilience is a process that requires time, effort, and a willingness to face difficult situations head-on.

One of the keys to developing resilience is to cultivate a growth mindset. This means viewing challenges as opportunities for growth and learning, rather than as insurmountable obstacles. It also involves focusing on what you can control, rather than on what you can't.

Another important aspect of resilience is building a support system. This can include friends, family, mentors, or professionals like therapists or coaches. Having people in your corner who can provide emotional support, guidance, and feedback can make all the difference in overcoming adversity.

Practicing self-care is also essential for developing resilience. This means taking care of your physical, emotional, and mental health. It can involve getting enough sleep, eating a healthy diet, engaging in regular exercise, and engaging in activities that bring you joy and fulfillment.

Finally, it's important to stay flexible and adaptable in the face of change. Resilience involves being able to adjust your plans and strategies when necessary, and to pivot when circumstances require it. This requires a willingness to take risks, try new things, and be open to different possibilities.

In summary, developing resilience is a crucial component of personal growth and success. By cultivating a growth mindset, building a support system, practicing self-care, and staying flexible and adaptable, you can become more resilient and better equipped to overcome life's challenges.

Developing resilience is a crucial skill that can help individuals navigate through difficult situations and bounce back from adversity. Resilience involves the ability to adapt to changes, cope with stress, and overcome obstacles. Here are some tips for developing resilience:

1. Build a support network: Having a support network of friends, family, or even professionals can help provide emotional support and encouragement during tough times.

2. Practice self-care: Taking care of yourself is important for maintaining resilience. This includes getting enough sleep, eating well, exercising regularly, and engaging in activities that bring you joy.

3. Develop a positive mindset: Cultivating a positive outlook can help you maintain resilience during difficult times. This includes reframing negative thoughts, practicing gratitude, and focusing on your strengths.

4. Set realistic goals: Setting realistic goals can help you maintain a sense of purpose and direction. Break down larger goals into smaller, manageable steps.

5. Practice problem-solving skills: Developing problem-solving skills can help you navigate through challenges and overcome obstacles. This includes identifying the problem, brainstorming solutions, and implementing a plan of action.

6. Learn from past experiences: Reflecting on past

experiences can help you learn from mistakes and build resilience. Ask yourself what you did well and what you could have done differently in previous challenging situations.

7. Embrace change: Change is a natural part of life, and learning to adapt to change can help build resilience. Instead of resisting change, try to embrace it as an opportunity for growth and learning.

8. Practice mindfulness: Mindfulness involves being present in the moment and paying attention to your thoughts and feelings without judgment. Practicing mindfulness can help reduce stress and improve emotional regulation, which are key components of resilience.

9. Seek out challenges: Challenging yourself can help build resilience by providing opportunities for personal growth and development. This can include taking on new responsibilities or trying new activities that push you out of your comfort zone.

10. Cultivate a sense of purpose: Having a sense of purpose and meaning can help you maintain resilience during difficult times. This can involve identifying your values and working towards goals that align with those values.

11. Practice self-compassion: Being kind to yourself is an important aspect of resilience. Treat yourself with the same care and compassion that you would offer to a friend who is struggling.

12. Develop problem-solving skills: When faced with challenges, it's important to have effective problem-solving skills. This includes breaking problems down into manageable steps, brainstorming potential solutions, and implementing a plan of action.

13. Seek out new experiences: Trying new things can help you build resilience by exposing you to a wider range of challenges and opportunities for growth.

14. Develop healthy coping mechanisms: Everyone copes with stress and challenges differently, but it's important to have healthy coping mechanisms that work for you. This might include exercise, meditation, journaling, or talking to a therapist.

15. Focus on the things you can control: When faced with difficult situations, it's easy to feel overwhelmed and powerless. Focusing on the things you can control can help you feel more empowered and resilient.

16. Practice gratitude: Cultivating a sense of gratitude can help you develop a more positive outlook and build resilience. Take time each day to focus on the things

in your life that you're grateful for, no matter how small they may be.

17. Stay connected: Maintaining social connections can help you build resilience by providing emotional support and a sense of community. This might involve spending time with loved ones, joining a support group, or volunteering in your community.

18. Take care of your mental health: Prioritizing your mental health is an important aspect of resilience. This might involve seeking help from a mental health professional, practicing stress-reduction techniques, or taking medication if needed.

19. Practice assertiveness: Learning to assert your needs and boundaries can help you build resilience by giving you a greater sense of control over your life. This might involve saying "no" to requests that you can't accommodate or standing up for yourself in difficult situations.

20. Keep learning and growing: Embracing a growth mindset can help you build resilience by fostering a sense of curiosity and a willingness to learn from experience. Make time to pursue new hobbies, learn new skills, or explore new interests.

Remember that resilience is not something you either have or don't have - it's a skill that can be developed and strengthened over time. By practicing these strategies consistently, you can build your resilience and become better equipped to handle life's challenges with confidence and grace.

Remember that developing resilience is an ongoing process, and it's okay to make mistakes along the way. By practicing these strategies consistently, you can build your resilience and become better equipped to handle life's challenges with grace and strength.

Chapter 9: Trying New Things

Trying new things is a key component of stepping outside your comfort zone. In this chapter, we'll look at the benefits of trying new things, and provide practical tips and strategies for doing so.

As humans, we are wired to seek out familiarity and routine. It is natural to want to stay within our comfort zone and avoid new experiences that may feel uncomfortable or unknown. However, trying new things is an essential aspect of personal growth and self-discovery.

When we try new things, we expand our horizons and expose ourselves to different perspectives and ways of living. It allows us to step outside of our own limited worldview and gain a broader understanding of the world around us.

Trying new things also helps us to develop our problem-solving skills and adaptability. When we are faced with unfamiliar situations, we are forced to think creatively and come up with innovative solutions to navigate them.

Furthermore, trying new things can be a source of joy and excitement in our lives. It provides us with new opportunities for fun and adventure, and can help us break out of monotonous routines.

Of course, trying new things can also be scary and intimidating. It may require us to face our fears or step outside of our comfort zone. However, the benefits far outweigh the potential discomfort. When we challenge ourselves to try new things, we build resilience and develop the confidence to face any obstacles that may come our way.

So, whether it's trying a new hobby, traveling to a new placc, or meeting new people, embrace the unknown and push yourself to try something new. You may be surprised at what you discover about yourself and the world around you.

When was the last time you tried something new? Perhaps it was a new hobby, a new food, or even a new way of thinking. Trying new things can be scary, but it can also be incredibly rewarding.

Stepping out of your comfort zone and trying new things can help you grow as a person, develop new skills, and gain new experiences. It can also help you overcome fear and resistance, and build confidence in yourself.

One way to start trying new things is to make a list of things you've always wanted to do or try, but have been too scared to attempt. Maybe you've always wanted to learn a new language, try a new sport, or start a new business. Write down these goals and make a plan to work towards them.

It's important to remember that trying new things doesn't always mean you'll succeed. In fact, you're likely to fail at some point. But failure isn't a reason to give up. Instead, it's an opportunity to learn and grow from your mistakes.

When you try new things, you also have the chance to meet new people and expand your network. You might find that you have a new passion or interest that you never would have discovered if you hadn't taken that first step.

So, the next time you're presented with an opportunity to try something new, take a chance and go for it. You never know where it might lead you.

Stepping outside of our comfort zones and trying new things can be a scary and intimidating experience, but it is also one of the most rewarding things we can do for ourselves.

When we stick to what we know and what feels safe, we limit

our growth and potential. However, when we challenge ourselves to try new things, we open ourselves up to a world of possibilities and opportunities.

It can be as simple as trying a new food or as complex as learning a new language or skill. Whatever it is, taking that first step outside of our comfort zone can be the hardest, but also the most important.

By pushing ourselves to try new things, we not only expand our knowledge and abilities, but we also build our confidence and resilience. We learn that we are capable of more than we thought, and that we can adapt and overcome challenges.

So next time you feel yourself hesitating to try something new, remember that the discomfort and uncertainty are temporary, but the growth and benefits can last a lifetime. Take that leap of faith and see where it takes you.

Chapter 10: Building a Support System

Stepping outside your comfort zone can be scary, but having a support system in place can make all the difference. In this chapter, we'll explore how to build a support system that will encourage and motivate you as you take on new challenges.

One of the most important aspects of personal growth is having a strong support system. Whether it's family, friends, mentors, or colleagues, having people who believe in you and encourage you can make all the difference in achieving your goals.

When we try to step outside our comfort zone and push ourselves to new limits, it can be intimidating and even scary. That's where having a support system can provide the motivation and reassurance we need to keep going.

A good support system should be made up of people who genuinely care about your success and well-being. They should be willing to offer guidance, feedback, and encouragement, while also holding you accountable and helping you stay focused on your goals.

It's important to build a support system that reflects your values and aspirations. Seek out people who share your passions and interests, and who can provide valuable insights and advice based on their own experiences.

Networking events, online forums, and professional associations can all be great places to meet like-minded people and build your support system. Don't be afraid to reach out to someone you admire or respect, and ask if they would be willing to offer their advice or mentorship.

Remember that building a support system is a two-way street. You should also be willing to offer your own support and encouragement to others who are working towards their own goals. By building a strong network of supportive people, you can not only achieve your own goals but also help others achieve theirs.

In summary, having a support system is crucial for personal growth and achieving your goals. Seek out people who share your values and passions, and be willing to offer your own support and encouragement in return. With the right support system in place, you can achieve anything you set your mind to.

Building a support system is crucial for stepping out of your comfort zone and pushing your limits. It's important to surround yourself with people who believe in you and support your goals. These people can help keep you accountable, encourage you when you feel discouraged, and offer advice when you need it.

Your support system doesn't have to be large, but it should be meaningful. It's better to have a few people who truly care about your success than a lot of people who don't. Your support system can include family members, friends, mentors, coaches, or anyone else who inspires you and encourages you to grow.

When building your support system, it's important to communicate your goals and needs clearly. Let your supporters know what you're working on and how they can help you. Be open to feedback and advice, but also be clear about your boundaries and what you're comfortable with.

Remember, building a support system is a two-way street. You should also be supportive of those in your network and offer help when you can. By building a strong support system, you create a community of like-minded individuals who can inspire each other to grow and achieve their goals.

Stepping outside of your comfort zone can be a challenging and rewarding experience, but it's important to have a support system in place to help you along the way. Here are some tips for building a support system that will help you push past your boundaries:

1. Identify your goals: Start by identifying the specific goals that you want to achieve. This will help you determine what kind of support you need and who can provide it.

2. Reach out to others: Don't be afraid to reach out to friends, family, and colleagues for support. Let them know about your goals and ask for their encouragement and assistance.

3. Join a community: Consider joining a group or community of like-minded individuals who share your interests or goals. This can provide you with a sense of belonging and support, as well as access to valuable resources and information.

4. Find a mentor: Seek out a mentor who has experience in the area you're trying to grow in. They can offer advice, guidance, and feedback to help you overcome challenges and achieve your goals.

5. Invest in self-care: Taking care of yourself is essential when stepping outside of your comfort zone. Make time for activities that help you relax and recharge, such as exercise, meditation, or hobbies.

Remember, building a support system takes time and effort, but it's worth it in the end. With the right people and resources in your corner, you can achieve anything you set your mind to.

Chapter 11: Embracing Discomfort

Discomfort is an inevitable part of stepping outside your comfort zone, but it doesn't have to be a negative experience. In this chapter, we'll look at how to embrace discomfort and use it as a catalyst for personal growth.

Discomfort is an inevitable part of life. We all face it at some point, whether it's physical discomfort from pushing ourselves too hard during a workout, or emotional discomfort from confronting our fears and insecurities. While it's tempting to avoid discomfort altogether, doing so can actually hold us back from reaching our full potential.

Instead of shying away from discomfort, we should embrace it as an opportunity for growth and learning. When we step out of our comfort zone and face challenges head-on, we build resilience and develop new skills that can benefit us in all areas of life.

One way to embrace discomfort is to start small. Choose a task that makes you slightly uncomfortable and challenge yourself to complete it. Maybe it's striking up a conversation with a stranger, trying a new hobby, or taking on a project at work that's outside your usual scope of responsibilities.

As you become more comfortable with discomfort, you can gradually increase the difficulty of the challenges you take on. The key is to approach discomfort with a growth mindset, viewing each experience as an opportunity to learn and improve.

It's also important to have a support system in place when facing discomfort. Surround yourself with people who encourage and motivate you to push past your limits. Seek out mentors or coaches who can offer guidance and support as you navigate new challenges.

Ultimately, embracing discomfort is about taking control of our lives and refusing to let fear and discomfort hold us back. By stepping outside our comfort zones and facing our fears head-on, we can build resilience, gain confidence, and achieve things we never thought possible.

When we encounter discomfort, it's natural to want to avoid it. But avoiding discomfort can also mean avoiding growth and progress. In order to expand our comfort zone and achieve our goals, we must learn to embrace discomfort.

One way to embrace discomfort is to change our perspective on it. Instead of seeing discomfort as a negative thing, we can see it as an opportunity to learn and grow. Discomfort is often a sign that we are stepping outside of our comfort zone and pushing ourselves to new heights.

Another way to embrace discomfort is to practice it intentionally. This could mean taking small steps outside of our comfort zone each day, or intentionally seeking out uncomfortable situations. For example, if we are uncomfortable with public speaking, we could seek out opportunities to practice speaking in front of others.

Finally, building resilience can also help us to embrace discomfort. By developing the skills and mindset to overcome challenges and adversity, we can become more comfortable with discomfort and better equipped to handle whatever comes our way.

Embracing discomfort may not always be easy, but it is necessary for personal growth and achieving our goals. By changing our perspective, practicing discomfort intentionally, and building resilience, we can learn to embrace discomfort and use it as a tool for growth and progress.

Embracing discomfort is an essential step towards getting out of your comfort zone. Comfort zones are those places or situations where you feel safe, secure, and familiar. While they may provide a sense of security, they can also prevent you from experiencing new things and taking risks.

By intentionally seeking out discomfort and challenging yourself to step outside your comfort zone, you can open yourself up to new opportunities for growth and learning. This might mean trying something new that you've never done before, taking on a challenging project at work, or engaging in a difficult conversation with someone.

It's important to remember that discomfort is not always a negative thing. In fact, it can be a sign that you're pushing yourself to grow and improve. Embracing discomfort can help you build resilience, increase your confidence, and develop new skills.

So, the next time you feel yourself slipping into your comfort zone, try to embrace discomfort instead. Seek out new challenges, take risks, and be open to learning from your experiences. With time and practice, you may find that stepping out of your comfort zone becomes easier and more rewarding.

As you begin to embrace discomfort, it's important to keep in mind that it's okay to fail. Failure is a natural part of the learning process and can be an opportunity to learn and grow. Don't let the fear of failure hold you back from taking risks and trying new things.

It can also be helpful to seek out support from others as you step out of your comfort zone. This might mean finding a mentor or accountability partner who can encourage you and provide guidance along the way.

Remember, the goal is not to constantly live outside of your comfort zone, but rather to expand it. As you challenge yourself and experience new things, you'll begin to see that what was once uncomfortable or unfamiliar has become more comfortable and familiar.

Finally, be patient with yourself as you work to embrace discomfort and get out of your comfort zone. Change and growth take time, and it's important to celebrate small victories along the way.

In conclusion, embracing discomfort can be a powerful tool for personal and professional growth. By stepping outside of your comfort zone and pushing yourself to try new things, you can build resilience, develop new skills, and unlock new opportunities for success.

Chapter 12: Cultivating a Growth Mindset

A growth mindset is the belief that your abilities and skills can be developed through hard work and dedication. In this chapter, we'll explore the benefits of a growth mindset, and provide tips for cultivating this mindset in your own life.

When it comes to achieving our goals and reaching our potential, having a growth mindset is crucial. A growth mindset is the belief that our abilities and intelligence can be developed and improved over time through hard work, perseverance, and learning from failures.

In contrast, a fixed mindset is the belief that our abilities and intelligence are static and cannot be changed, leading to a fear of failure and a reluctance to take on new challenges.

Cultivating a growth mindset involves adopting certain attitudes and behaviors that can help us reach our full potential:

1. Embrace challenges: Rather than avoiding challenges or giving up when things get difficult, embrace them as opportunities for growth and learning.

2. Learn from failures: Instead of seeing failures as setbacks or evidence of our limitations, use them as opportunities to learn and improve.

3. Persist through obstacles: Instead of giving up when faced with obstacles or setbacks, persevere and keep pushing forward.

4. Seek out feedback: Rather than being defensive or resistant to feedback, actively seek it out as a way to learn and grow.

5. Emphasize effort over innate ability: Instead of believing that success is solely based on innate ability or talent, focus on the effort and hard work required to achieve your goals.

By cultivating a growth mindset, we can overcome the limitations of a fixed mindset and achieve our full potential in all areas of life. With perseverance, hard work, and a willingness to learn and grow, we can overcome challenges and achieve success beyond what we ever thought possible.

To cultivate a growth mindset, it's important to embrace challenges, view mistakes as opportunities to learn and grow, and persist in the face of setbacks. It's about believing that your abilities and intelligence can be developed with effort and dedication, rather than being fixed traits.

One way to develop a growth mindset is to focus on the process rather than just the outcome. This means valuing the effort, hard work, and progress that you make along the way, rather than just the end result. It also means being willing to try new things, take risks, and learn from failures.

Another key component of a growth mindset is self-reflection. This involves taking the time to reflect on your experiences, strengths, weaknesses, and goals, and using this information to make positive changes in your life. It also involves being open to feedback and criticism, and using it to improve yourself and your performance.

Finally, cultivating a growth mindset means embracing a love of learning. This means being curious, seeking out new knowledge and experiences, and constantly challenging yourself to learn and grow. It means being willing to push yourself out of your comfort zone and embrace new opportunities, even if they are difficult or scary.

By cultivating a growth mindset, you can transform your life and achieve your goals, no matter how challenging or daunting they may seem. So take the time to reflect on your beliefs and attitudes, and start making positive changes today. Cultivating a growth mindset is essential for getting out of one's comfort zone because it helps individuals to view challenges and failures as opportunities for learning and growth. People with a growth mindset believe that their abilities and intelligence can be developed through hard work, persistence, and dedication.

In contrast, those with a fixed mindset believe that their abilities are predetermined and unchangeable, leading them to avoid challenges and shy away from risks that could lead to growth and improvement.

When individuals embrace a growth mindset, they are more likely to take risks and step outside of their comfort zones, as they see challenges and failures as opportunities to learn and develop new skills. They are also more likely to seek out feedback and use it constructively to improve their performance.

By getting out of their comfort zones and taking on new challenges, individuals can expand their knowledge and abilities, gain confidence, and achieve personal and professional growth. This growth mindset also helps individuals to overcome the fear of failure, which can hold them back from reaching their full potential.

In summary, cultivating a growth mindset is crucial for individuals who want to break out of their comfort zones and achieve personal and professional growth. It helps people to view challenges and failures as opportunities for learning, embrace risks and seek out feedback, and overcome the fear of failure.

A growth mindset is the belief that our abilities and intelligence can be developed through dedication and hard work. It is the opposite of a fixed mindset, which assumes that our abilities and intelligence are fixed traits that cannot be changed.

If you want to get rid of your comfort zone and cultivate a growth mindset, there are a few things you can do.

1. Embrace challenges: Instead of avoiding challenges, embrace them. Challenge yourself to try new things and take on tasks that are outside of your comfort zone. This will help you grow and develop new skills.

2. Learn from failures: Instead of being discouraged by failure, see it as an opportunity to learn and grow. Analyze what went wrong and figure out what you can do differently next time.

3. Persist through obstacles: When you encounter

obstacles, don't give up. Keep pushing through and working hard. This will help you develop resilience and perseverance.

4. Believe in yourself: Develop a strong sense of self-belief. Believe that you can learn and grow, and that you are capable of achieving great things.

5. Embrace the learning process: Instead of focusing solely on the end result, embrace the learning process. Enjoy the journey of growth and development, and appreciate the small victories along the way.

6. Surround yourself with growth-minded individuals: Surrounding yourself with people who have a growth mindset can be incredibly helpful. They can provide support and encouragement, and can inspire you to continue pushing yourself outside of your comfort zone.

7. Practice self-reflection: Take time to reflect on your progress and identify areas where you can improve. This will help you stay on track and continue growing.

8. Set achievable goals: Setting achievable goals can help you stay motivated and focused. Break down larger goals into smaller, more manageable steps, and celebrate each accomplishment along the way.

9. Take calculated risks: Taking calculated risks can help you grow and develop new skills. Evaluate the risks and benefits of a particular decision, and make a plan to mitigate any potential negative outcomes.

10. Continuously learn and seek new opportunities: Continuously learning and seeking new opportunities can help you stay motivated and inspired. Attend workshops, read books, and seek out mentors who can help you continue to grow and develop.

11. Practice mindfulness: Practicing mindfulness can help you stay present and focused, which is essential for developing a growth mindset. By staying in the present moment, you can avoid getting overwhelmed by past failures or future uncertainties.

12. Celebrate progress, not just success: Celebrate your progress, even if you haven't achieved your ultimate goal yet. By focusing on your progress, you can stay motivated and inspired, even when things get tough.

13. Stay flexible and adaptable: A growth mindset requires flexibility and adaptability. Be open to new ideas and ways of doing things, and be willing to adjust your approach if necessary.

14. Avoid negative self-talk: Negative self-talk can be a major barrier to developing a growth mindset. Instead

of beating yourself up for mistakes or setbacks, focus on the positive aspects of your journey and how you can learn from your experiences.

15. Practice gratitude: Practicing gratitude can help you stay positive and focused on the good things in your life. Take time each day to reflect on what you're grateful for, and focus on the positive aspects of your growth and development.

By incorporating these practices into your daily life, you can cultivate a growth mindset and achieve your goals, even when things get tough. Remember, developing a growth mindset is a process that takes time and dedication, but with persistence and a willingness to learn, you can unlock your full potential and achieve great things.

Chapter 13: Finding Joy in the Journey

Stepping outside your comfort zone can be challenging, but it can also be a source of joy and fulfillment. In this chapter, we'll look at how to find joy in the journey, and appreciate the process of personal growth.

Life is not just about the destination, but it's also about the journey. In this chapter, we explore the importance of finding joy in the journey of stepping outside our comfort zones.

When we push ourselves out of our comfort zones, we can easily become fixated on the end goal. We may think that happiness and fulfillment will only come once we have achieved what we set out to do. But the truth is that happiness and fulfillment can be found in every step we take towards our goals.

The journey towards personal growth and development can be challenging, but it can also be incredibly rewarding. It's about the small victories along the way, the moments of self-discovery, and the growth we experience as we face our fears and overcome obstacles.

When we cultivate a mindset of joy and gratitude for the journey, we allow ourselves to appreciate the present moment and find meaning in every experience. We become more resilient, more adaptable, and more open to new opportunities.

So, rather than focusing solely on the destination, let's learn to enjoy the journey. Let's celebrate every small victory, embrace every challenge, and find joy in the process of stepping outside our comfort zones. Let's cultivate a growth mindset that allows us to see every experience as an opportunity for growth and learning.

By doing so, we can find fulfillment not just in achieving our goals, but in the journey that leads us there.

As you embark on your journey of growth and self-improvement, it is important to remember that the destination is not the only thing that matters. Finding joy in the journey itself is crucial for maintaining motivation and sustaining progress.

It's easy to get caught up in the idea of achieving a certain goal or reaching a particular destination. We may think that once we get there, we will finally be happy and fulfilled. But the truth is, happiness and fulfillment can be found in the everyday moments of the journey.

Take the time to appreciate the progress you've made, no matter how small. Celebrate the small victories and find joy in the process of pushing yourself beyond your comfort zone. Embrace the challenges and setbacks as opportunities for growth and learning.

Remember to be kind to yourself along the way. Don't beat yourself up for mistakes or failures. Instead, use them as opportunities for reflection and growth. Cultivate self-compassion and gratitude for the progress you've made and the support system that surrounds you.

Ultimately, finding joy in the journey is about cultivating a positive mindset and focusing on the present moment. Enjoy the process of becoming the best version of yourself and the small moments that make up your journey. With this mindset, you can create a fulfilling and meaningful life, no matter where your journey takes you.

Getting out of your comfort zone can be challenging, but it

can also be a rewarding and fulfilling experience. Instead of focusing solely on the end result or destination, it's important to find joy in the journey itself.

One way to do this is by setting small goals and celebrating each accomplishment along the way. By breaking down a big goal into smaller, more manageable steps, you can make the process feel less overwhelming and more enjoyable.

Another way to find joy in the journey is by embracing the unknown and being open to new experiences. When you step out of your comfort zone, you're opening yourself up to opportunities and experiences that you may not have otherwise had. Even if things don't go exactly as planned, you can learn and grow from each experience.

It's also important to remember that getting out of your comfort zone doesn't mean you have to do something extreme or risky. It can be as simple as trying a new hobby or activity, speaking up in a meeting, or having a conversation with someone new.

Finally, don't forget to give yourself grace and be kind to yourself throughout the process. It's okay to make mistakes or feel uncomfortable at times. Recognize that growth and progress often come with discomfort and challenge, and trust that you have the ability to handle whatever comes your way.

In summary, finding joy in the journey of getting out of your comfort zone involves setting small goals, embracing the unknown, being open to new experiences, being kind to yourself, and celebrating each accomplishment along the way.

Chapter 14: Maintaining Momentum

Once you've started stepping outside your comfort zone, it's important to maintain momentum and continue to push yourself. In this chapter, we'll explore strategies for maintaining momentum, and avoiding the temptation to slip back into old habits.

Maintaining momentum is crucial in achieving our goals and continuing to push ourselves outside our comfort zones. After taking the initial steps to step out of our comfort zones, it can be easy to fall back into old habits and routines.

To avoid this, it is important to establish a routine and maintain consistency. This can be done by setting regular goals and creating a schedule to accomplish them. By doing this, we can build momentum and create a sense of progress, which can help us stay motivated and focused.

It is also important to celebrate small wins along the way. Recognizing and celebrating our accomplishments, no matter how small, can help us maintain our momentum and stay motivated to continue pushing ourselves.

Additionally, it is important to remain open to new experiences and challenges. Being open-minded and willing to learn from new experiences can help us continue to grow and maintain momentum.

Finally, it is important to surround ourselves with supportive and encouraging individuals who can help us stay motivated and accountable. Building a strong support system can help us maintain our momentum and achieve our goals.

As you continue to push past your comfort zone, it's important to remember to maintain momentum. This means consistently challenging yourself and seeking out new experiences, even when it becomes difficult or scary. It's easy to get comfortable again once you've achieved some level of success, but that can lead to complacency and a lack of progress.

To maintain momentum, it can be helpful to set new goals for yourself and create a plan for how you will achieve them. This plan should include specific steps you will take, as well as deadlines to hold yourself accountable. You may also find it helpful to track your progress and celebrate your successes along the way.

Another important aspect of maintaining momentum is learning from your failures and setbacks. Instead of getting discouraged or giving up, use these experiences as opportunities to grow and improve. Reflect on what went wrong and what you can do differently next time to achieve better results.

Remember that the journey is never over, and there is always room for growth and improvement. By maintaining momentum and embracing the challenges that come your way, you can continue to expand your comfort zone and achieve your full potential.

Maintaining momentum is crucial for getting out of your comfort zone because it helps you build the necessary momentum to push through the discomfort and fear that often accompany stepping outside of what feels familiar and safe.

When you're in your comfort zone, you're typically doing things that are familiar and easy. While this may feel good in the moment, it can also limit your growth and prevent you from reaching your full potential.

To break out of your comfort zone, you need to be willing to take risks and try new things, even if they make you feel uncomfortable or uncertain. Maintaining momentum can help you do this by providing a sense of forward motion and progress that can be motivating and energizing.

By setting small goals and consistently taking steps towards them, you can build momentum and gain confidence in your ability to handle new challenges. Over time, this can help you develop a sense of resilience and adaptability that will serve you well as you continue to push yourself outside of your comfort zone.

So if you're looking to get out of your comfort zone, remember to focus on maintaining momentum by setting small, achievable goals and consistently taking action towards them. With time and practice, you'll find that stepping outside of your comfort zone becomes easier and more rewarding, and you'll be able to achieve things you never thought possible.

Additionally, maintaining momentum can also help you develop a growth mindset. Instead of seeing challenges and failures as signs of weakness or incompetence, you'll begin to view them as opportunities for learning and growth.

This mindset shift can be transformative, as it allows you to approach new experiences with curiosity and openness, rather than fear and resistance. It can also help you bounce back more quickly from setbacks and failures, as you'll be more focused on the lessons learned than the negative emotions associated with the experience.

To maintain momentum, it's important to stay accountable to yourself and your goals. This can mean finding an accountability partner, joining a group of like-minded individuals, or simply setting reminders and deadlines for yourself.

It's also important to celebrate your successes, no matter how small they may seem. Celebrating your progress can help you stay motivated and reinforce the positive changes you're making in your life.

In summary, maintaining momentum is essential for getting out of your comfort zone and achieving your goals. By setting small goals, staying accountable, and celebrating your successes, you can build the momentum you need to push through discomfort and fear, develop a growth mindset, and unlock your full potential.

Chapter 15: Making Stepping Outside Your Comfort Zone a Habit

Stepping outside your comfort zone shouldn't be a one-time event - it should be a habit that you cultivate over time. In this chapter, we'll provide practical tips for making stepping outside your comfort zone a regular part of your life, and reaping the rewards of personal growth and fulfillment.

Congratulations on taking the steps to step outside of your comfort zone and embrace growth and change! But remember, stepping outside of your comfort zone is not a one-time event. It's a journey that requires consistent effort and dedication. Making it a habit can be challenging, but it is essential for long-term personal and professional growth.

Here are some tips to help you make stepping outside your comfort zone a habit:

1. Create a routine: Incorporate stepping outside your comfort zone into your daily routine. This could be something as simple as talking to a stranger, trying a new food, or taking a different route to work.

2. Set achievable goals: Set realistic goals for stepping outside your comfort zone, and ensure that they are measurable and achievable. This will help you stay motivated and track your progress.

3. Celebrate small wins: Celebrate your small wins and milestones. Recognize that every step you take towards your goal is progress.

4. Hold yourself accountable: Hold yourself accountable for stepping outside your comfort zone. This could be done by keeping a journal or working with a coach or accountability partner.

5. Embrace failure: Embrace failure as an opportunity to learn and grow. Remember that failure is a part of the growth process and not a sign of defeat.

6. Practice self-care: Taking care of yourself is essential to maintaining momentum and making stepping outside your comfort zone a habit. Ensure that you are getting enough rest, eating a healthy diet, and engaging in activities that bring you joy.

Remember, stepping outside your comfort zone is not easy, but it is worth it. With time and practice, it will become easier, and you will be amazed at the personal and professional growth you experience. Keep pushing yourself, and you will be amazed at what you can achieve.

To make stepping outside your comfort zone a habit, it's important to set realistic goals, track your progress, and celebrate your successes along the way. You may also want to consider incorporating some of the following strategies into your daily routine:

1. Start small: Begin by taking small steps outside of your comfort zone, and gradually work your way up to bigger challenges.

2. Build on past successes: Reflect on times when you have successfully stepped outside of your comfort zone in the past, and use those experiences as motivation to keep going.

3. Surround yourself with support: Seek out friends, family members, or mentors who will encourage and support you as you take on new challenges.

4. Make it a regular practice: Schedule regular times to step outside your comfort zone, such as once a week or once a month, and hold yourself accountable to following through.

5. Embrace discomfort: Recognize that discomfort is a natural part of growth and learning, and try to reframe

uncomfortable situations as opportunities for growth.

By incorporating these strategies into your daily life, you can gradually build the habit of stepping outside your comfort zone and reap the rewards of personal growth and development. Remember, the journey outside your comfort zone may be challenging at times, but the rewards are well worth the effort.

Stepping outside of your comfort zone can be a valuable habit to cultivate for a number of reasons. When you remain within your comfort zone, you tend to stick to familiar patterns and routines, which can limit your growth and prevent you from reaching your full potential.

On the other hand, when you intentionally seek out new experiences and challenges, you can expand your horizons and develop new skills and perspectives. This can help you become more adaptable, resilient, and open-minded, which can be valuable qualities in both your personal and professional life.

Stepping outside your comfort zone can also help you overcome fears and insecurities. By taking on challenges that push you beyond what you're used to, you can develop greater self-confidence and a stronger sense of self-efficacy.

Of course, stepping outside your comfort zone can also be uncomfortable or even scary at times. But with practice, you can learn to embrace the discomfort and use it as a catalyst for growth and self-improvement. And the more you do it, the easier it will become.

Overall, making stepping outside your comfort zone a habit can help you live a more fulfilling and meaningful life, and can help you reach your full potential.

Additionally, stepping outside of your comfort zone can lead to new opportunities and experiences that you may have never encountered otherwise. By trying new things and taking on new challenges, you may discover hidden talents or passions that you never knew you had.

For example, if you're used to sticking to a particular routine in your personal or professional life, you may miss out on opportunities to connect with new people, learn new skills, or try new things. But by stepping outside your comfort zone and trying something different, you may discover a new hobby or interest that brings you joy and fulfillment.

Furthermore, stepping outside of your comfort zone can also improve your problem-solving skills. When you encounter new and unfamiliar situations, you are forced to think creatively and come up with new solutions. This can help you develop a more flexible and adaptive mindset, which can be a valuable asset in both your personal and professional life.

In conclusion, while stepping outside of your comfort zone may seem daunting at first, the benefits of doing so can be tremendous. By making it a habit to push yourself beyond your limits and try new things, you can expand your horizons, grow as a person, and live a more fulfilling life. So don't be afraid to take that first step – you never know what opportunities and experiences may be waiting for you.

Chapter 16: Mentorship

Mentorship can play a valuable role in helping individuals step out of their comfort zones. A mentor can provide guidance, support, and encouragement as someone navigates unfamiliar territory, which can help to build confidence and reduce anxiety.

One way a mentor can support someone in expanding their comfort zone is by challenging them to take on new experiences or try new things. This can be done in a safe and supportive way, with the mentor providing advice and feedback along the way.

Another important role of a mentor is to help someone identify and address limiting beliefs or thought patterns that may be holding them back from expanding their comfort zone. By working with a mentor to challenge these beliefs and shift their perspective, someone can gain greater resilience and adaptability when faced with new challenges.

Ultimately, the role of a mentor in relation to comfort zones is to help someone move beyond their current limitations and realize their full potential. With the right support and guidance, individuals can develop the skills and confidence they need to tackle new challenges and achieve their goals.

Another way that mentorship can be helpful in expanding comfort zones is by providing accountability. A mentor can help someone set goals and work towards them, checking in regularly to provide support and encouragement. This can help someone stay motivated and focused on their goals, even when they encounter obstacles or setbacks.

In addition, a mentor can serve as a role model for stepping out of one's comfort zone. By sharing their own experiences and challenges, a mentor can inspire someone to take risks and try new things. This can be particularly helpful if the mentee lacks confidence or is hesitant to take action on their own.

Overall, mentorship can be a powerful tool for expanding comfort zones and helping individuals reach their full potential. By providing guidance, support, and accountability, a mentor can help someone build resilience and adaptability, and develop the skills they need to succeed in any situation.

A mentor can provide constructive feedback on someone's progress, helping them identify areas for improvement and providing guidance on how to overcome obstacles. This can be particularly valuable when someone is working to expand their comfort zone, as they may be unsure of how to navigate new challenges.

Reflection is also an important part of the mentorship process. By regularly reflecting on their experiences and progress, someone can gain insight into their strengths and weaknesses, and develop a deeper understanding of themselves. This self-awareness can be a powerful tool for expanding comfort zones, as it can help someone identify areas where they need to push themselves further, and areas where they may be holding themselves back.

In addition, mentorship can help someone build a network of support and resources. A mentor can introduce someone to new people and opportunities, and help them navigate unfamiliar situations. This can be particularly helpful when someone is trying to expand their comfort zone, as it can provide a sense of community and help them feel more confident and supported.

Overall, mentorship is a valuable tool for expanding comfort zones and helping individuals grow and develop. By providing guidance, support, and feedback, a mentor can help someone overcome their fears and take on new challenges, ultimately leading to greater success and fulfillment.

A mentor can provide a sounding board for ideas and strategies, helping someone to identify the most effective ways to approach new challenges. This can be particularly helpful when someone is stepping outside of their comfort zone, as they may be unsure of how to proceed or what to expect.

Mentorship can also help someone develop important life skills, such as communication, problem-solving, and resilience. By working with a mentor, someone can learn how to effectively navigate difficult situations, communicate their ideas and needs, and adapt to changing circumstances.

Overall, mentorship is a valuable tool for expanding comfort zones and helping individuals reach their full potential. By providing guidance, support, and expertise, a mentor can help someone overcome their fears and take on new challenges, ultimately leading to greater success and fulfillment.

One important aspect of mentorship is the opportunity for someone to develop a growth mindset. A growth mindset is the belief that one's abilities and skills can be developed through hard work and dedication. This mindset can be especially helpful when someone is trying to expand their comfort zone, as it can help them approach new challenges with a sense of optimism and determination.

A mentor can help someone develop a growth mindset by providing encouragement and support, and by helping them set realistic goals that can be achieved through effort and perseverance. By focusing on the process of learning and growth, rather than just the outcome, a mentor can help someone develop a sense of confidence and resilience that can carry over into other areas of their life.

In addition, mentorship can help someone develop a sense of self-efficacy, or the belief in one's ability to accomplish tasks and achieve goals. By working with a mentor to set and achieve goals, someone can develop a sense of accomplishment and mastery that can help them tackle new challenges and expand their comfort zone.

ABOUT THE AUTHOR

Badairnath Devarasetty is started carier with employee having 15+ years of experience. He did masters from Indian Instute of Technolodge, Madras. He has mentored more than 50+ people and guided them for Social Entraprnuer .

REFERENCES

- Goals!: How to Get Everything You Want Faster Than You Ever Thought Possible By Brian Tracy

- Mindset: The New Psychology of Success by Carol S. Dweck (Author)

- The Growth Mindset: A Guide to Professional and Personal Growth by Joshua Moore (Author), Helen Glasgow (Author)

- Think and Grow Rich Book by Napoleon Hill

- The Magic of Thinking Big Book by David J. Schwartz

www.ingramcontent.com/pod-product-compliance
Lightning Source LLC
Chambersburg PA
CBHW070844160726
48004CB00001B/496